DRAWING FUN

ACKNOWLEDGEMENT

The authors, Carolyn Davis and Charlene Brown, would like to thank all of the following for their patience and support; Sally Black, Sally Marshall Corngold, Cheri LeClear, John Raley, Pat Brown and our friends at Marian Bergeson Elementary and of course, the wonderful staff at Walter Foster Publishing, Inc.

INTRODUCTION

Drawing can be easy and fun. With a few tips and a little practice you can draw anything.

In this book, we will show you how to draw anything using shapes you already know.

We will also show you how to use tracing paper as a way to develop your drawing skills. By tracing, you will learn how to draw your favorite cartoon, drawing or photo.

In chapters four, five and six you will learn how to use shading, shadows, and perspective to make your drawings more life like.

We want you to remember as you use this book, there are no right or wrong ways to draw. Everyone has their own creative style and imagination.

You must decide for yourself how you want your drawings to look. We can, however, give you tips that will make drawing easier.

Most importantly, as you learn from this book, we want you to enjoy drawing.

Please, **have fun!**

GLOSSARY

Detail—A small part of the whole picture. Detail can be buttons, bows, furry texture, eyes, shadows, etc.

Horizon—The line where the sky and earth seem to meet. Notice that the horizon always seems to be at your eye level. In art, the horizon line is used as a guide for perspective.

Light Source—The sun, a lamp, a window or any place from which light begins or comes through. In art, knowing your light source will help you know where shadows and shading should be to make your drawing look real.

Overlapping—One object resting on top or in front of another object, partially covering the object up. In art, overlapping is used to make objects look closer or further away.

Point of Perspective—The way things appear from where you are looking. In art, you draw from your point of perspective.

Pressure—The amount of strength used to apply one object to another. In art, if you want an object to appear dark you apply more pressure on your drawing tool. If you want an object to appear light you apply less pressure.

Shading—The use of black or color to give the effect of shade or shadows in a picture.

Texture—The way something looks or feels. An object can have a furry texture, a smooth texture, a rough texture, etc. In art, drawing in texture makes the object look more real.

Values—In art, value is the degree of lightness or darkness.

Vanishing Point—The point at which something seems to disappear into the horizon. For example, the point at which railroad tracks seem to disappear off into the distance.

4.

CONTENTS

MATERIALS

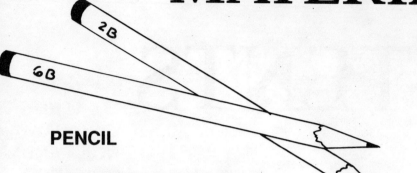

PENCIL

THERE ARE HARD PENCILS
(MARKED WITH A "**H**")
AND SOFT LEAD PENCILS
(MARKED WITH A "**B**")
SOFT LEAD PENCILS ARE EASIEST
TO USE. WE RECOMMEND SOFT
PENCILS MARKED 2B OR 3B.
2B PENCILS ARE THE MOST
COMMON

RULER

USED FOR MEASURING AND MAK-
ING STRAIGHT LINES.

CHARCOAL

BLACK CHARCOAL STICKS COME IN
THICK OR THIN SIZES.

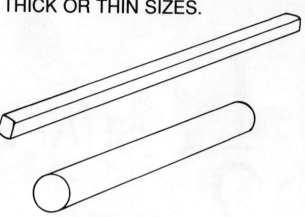

QUILL PENS

QUILL PENS ARE OLD FASHIONED
TOOLS USED FOR INK DRAWING. YO
CAN GET DIFFERENT SIZE AND
SHAPE TIPS TO MAKE DIFFERENT
LOOKING LINES.

FELT TIP PENS

THERE ARE MANY KINDS: FINE
POINT, WIDE TIPS, WATER BASE,
PERMANENT INK. THESE ARE ALSO
CALLED MARKING PENS OR ART
MARKERS.

MATERIALS

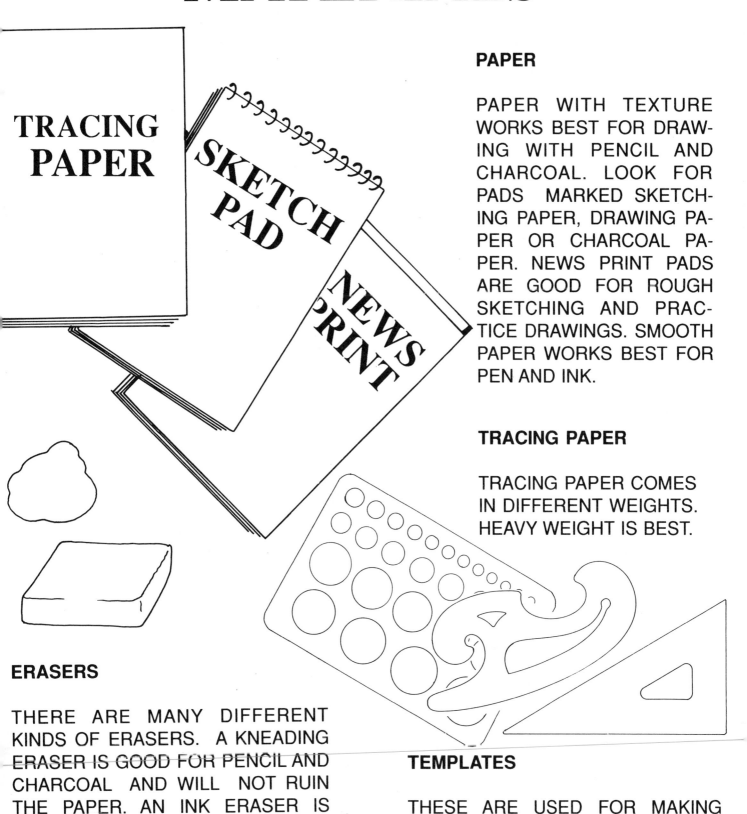

TRACING PAPER

SKETCH PAD

NEWS PRINT

PAPER

PAPER WITH TEXTURE WORKS BEST FOR DRAWING WITH PENCIL AND CHARCOAL. LOOK FOR PADS MARKED SKETCHING PAPER, DRAWING PAPER OR CHARCOAL PAPER. NEWS PRINT PADS ARE GOOD FOR ROUGH SKETCHING AND PRACTICE DRAWINGS. SMOOTH PAPER WORKS BEST FOR PEN AND INK.

TRACING PAPER

TRACING PAPER COMES IN DIFFERENT WEIGHTS. HEAVY WEIGHT IS BEST.

ERASERS

THERE ARE MANY DIFFERENT KINDS OF ERASERS. A KNEADING ERASER IS GOOD FOR PENCIL AND CHARCOAL AND WILL NOT RUIN THE PAPER. AN INK ERASER IS GOOD FOR PEN AND INK AND WILL ERASE ON SMOOTH PAPER WITHOUT TEARING.

TEMPLATES

THESE ARE USED FOR MAKING PERFECT CIRCLES, OVALS, CURVES AND OTHER SHAPES. THESE COME IN MANY DIFFERENT DESIGNS.

7.

8.

SHAPES ARE FUN

Triangle, circle, square - you know all the basic shapes. But do you know that these are the same shapes that professional artists use to draw animals, houses - anything!

Chapter One shows you how to put together different shapes to make fun drawings.

Once you see how shapes form objects, you will start to notice shapes in everything around you at school, on your way home, everywhere.

You may discover that a cat is two circles, two triangles, and a tail. The best way to use this chapter is by drawing the shapes on pages ten and eleven. Create drawings using either our examples or your own imagination.

The examples we give are just our ideas - you may have totally different ideas of what a clown or a cat should look like. Neither is right or wrong. They are just different ways to look at the same thing.

Most importantly; **have fun** coming up with different ways to use basic shapes!

IF YOU CAN DRAW OR TRACE THESE SHAPES...

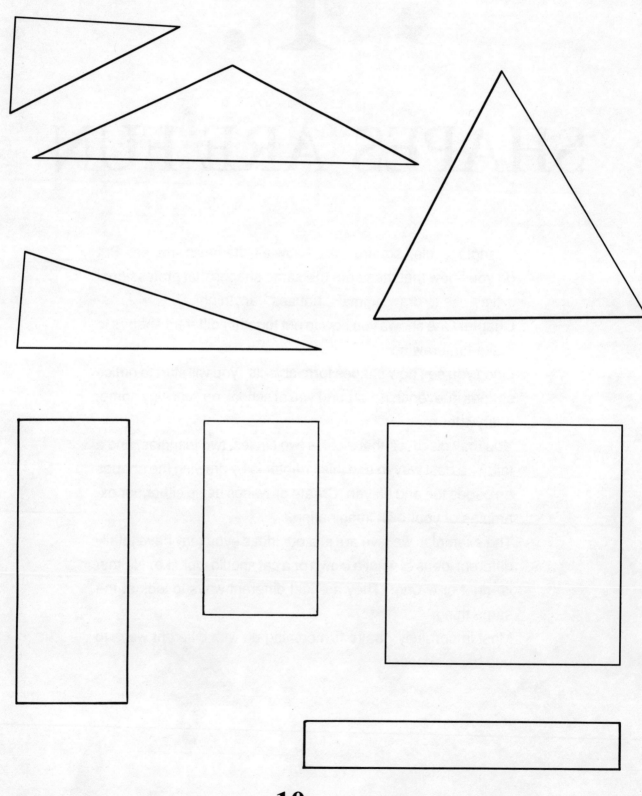

**...YOU CAN DRAW A FURRY FRIEND,
A SCARY MONSTER, OR A PLACE TO GO!**

11.

12.

SEE THE SHAPES

**TRACE A TREE, A COTTAGE,
A BRIGHT, SHINING SUN...
ALL OF A SUDDEN-
DRAWING IS FUN!**

YOU CAN DRAW

14.

ANYTHING WITH SHAPES

16.

2.

MORE SHAPES

USE SHAPES TO DRAW IN SIX EASY STEPS

Chapter Two shows how to put a variety of shapes together to make more fun drawings. In addition to using the shapes in Chapter One, you can see how to overlap shapes to make more realistic drawings. You may want to trace these shapes.

Tracing with pen over your pencil lines will make it easier for you to see how drawings are made of overlapping shapes.

After you have drawn the shapes you need, you can add in as much detail as you want.

You'll see that each drawing only takes six easy steps.

Once again, **have fun**! Remember, shapes can be used to put your imagination on paper.

DRAW A DOG

1. DRAW SHAPES IN LIGHT PENCIL.

2. USING PEN OR FELT TIP PEN, DRAW OVER THE LINES YOU WANT TO KEEP.

3. ERASE LIGHT PENCIL.

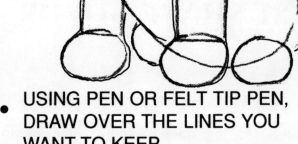

4. DRAW DETAILS IN LIGHT PENCIL.

5. USING PEN OR FELT TIP PEN, DRAW IN DETAILS.

6. ERASE LIGHT PENCIL.

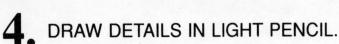

18.

OR CAT IN 6 EASY STEPS

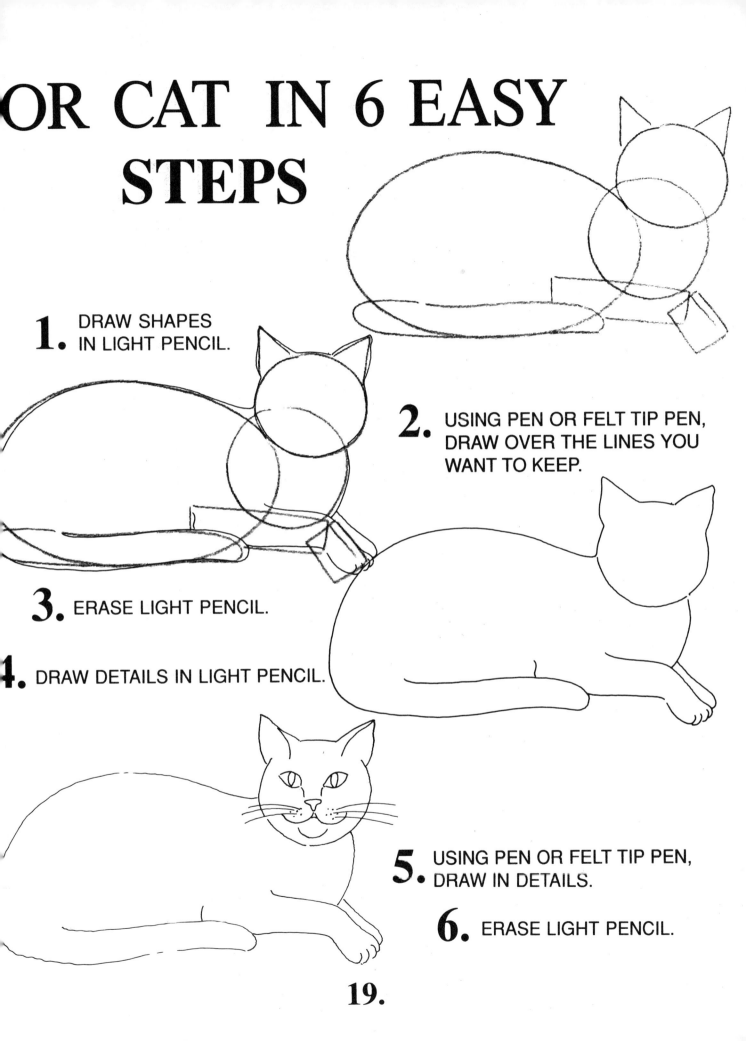

1. DRAW SHAPES IN LIGHT PENCIL.

2. USING PEN OR FELT TIP PEN, DRAW OVER THE LINES YOU WANT TO KEEP.

3. ERASE LIGHT PENCIL.

4. DRAW DETAILS IN LIGHT PENCIL.

5. USING PEN OR FELT TIP PEN, DRAW IN DETAILS.

6. ERASE LIGHT PENCIL.

19.

BOATS

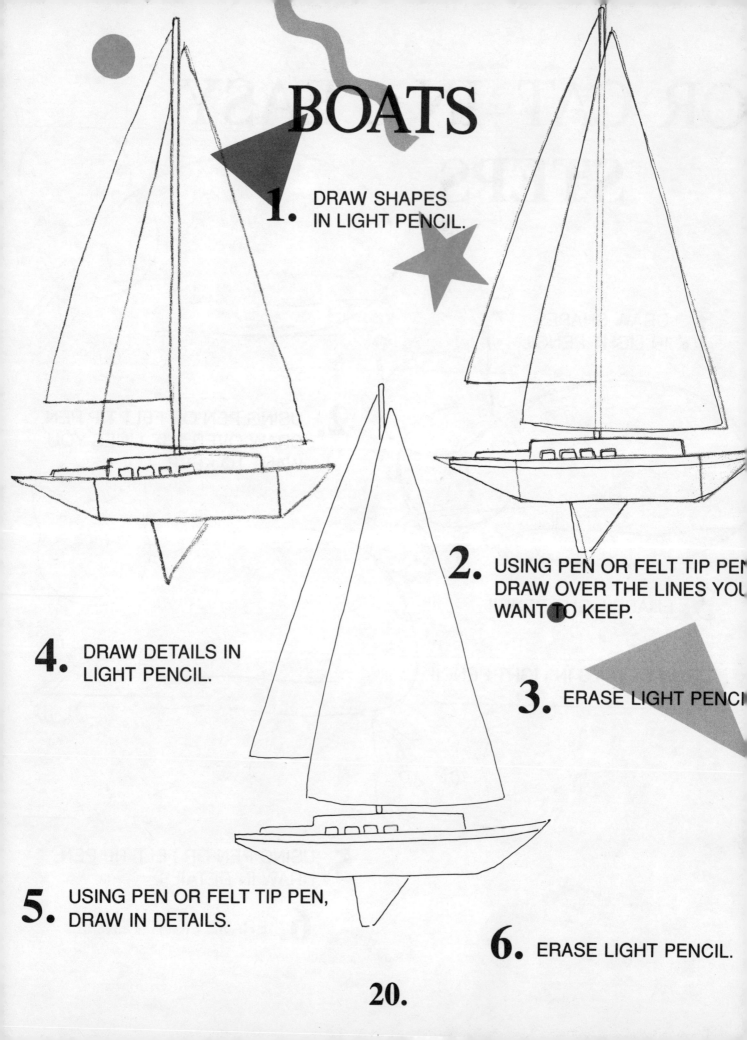

1. DRAW SHAPES IN LIGHT PENCIL.

2. USING PEN OR FELT TIP PEN DRAW OVER THE LINES YOU WANT TO KEEP.

3. ERASE LIGHT PENCIL

4. DRAW DETAILS IN LIGHT PENCIL.

5. USING PEN OR FELT TIP PEN, DRAW IN DETAILS.

6. ERASE LIGHT PENCIL.

20.

OR BEARS

1. DRAW SHAPES IN LIGHT PENCIL.

2. USING PEN OR FELT TIP PEN, DRAW OVER THE LINES YOU WANT TO KEEP.

3. ERASE LIGHT PENCIL.

4. DRAW DETAILS IN LIGHT PENCIL.

5. USING PEN OR FELT TIP PEN, DRAW IN DETAILS.

6. ERASE LIGHT PENCIL.

21.

HELICOPTERS

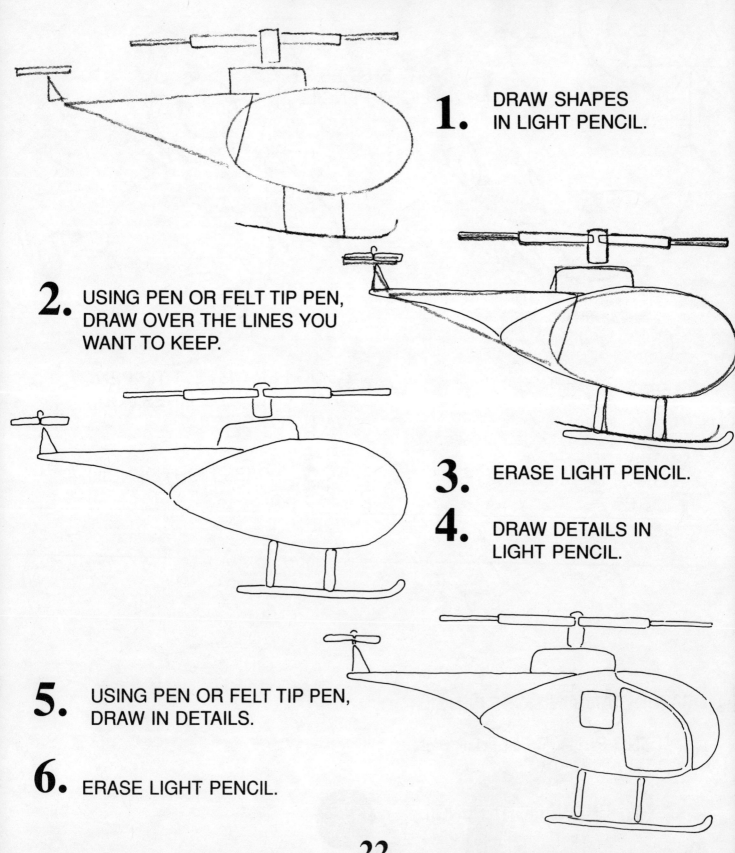

1. DRAW SHAPES
IN LIGHT PENCIL.

2. USING PEN OR FELT TIP PEN,
DRAW OVER THE LINES YOU
WANT TO KEEP.

3. ERASE LIGHT PENCIL.

4. DRAW DETAILS IN
LIGHT PENCIL.

5. USING PEN OR FELT TIP PEN,
DRAW IN DETAILS.

6. ERASE LIGHT PENCIL.

AND DINOSAURS

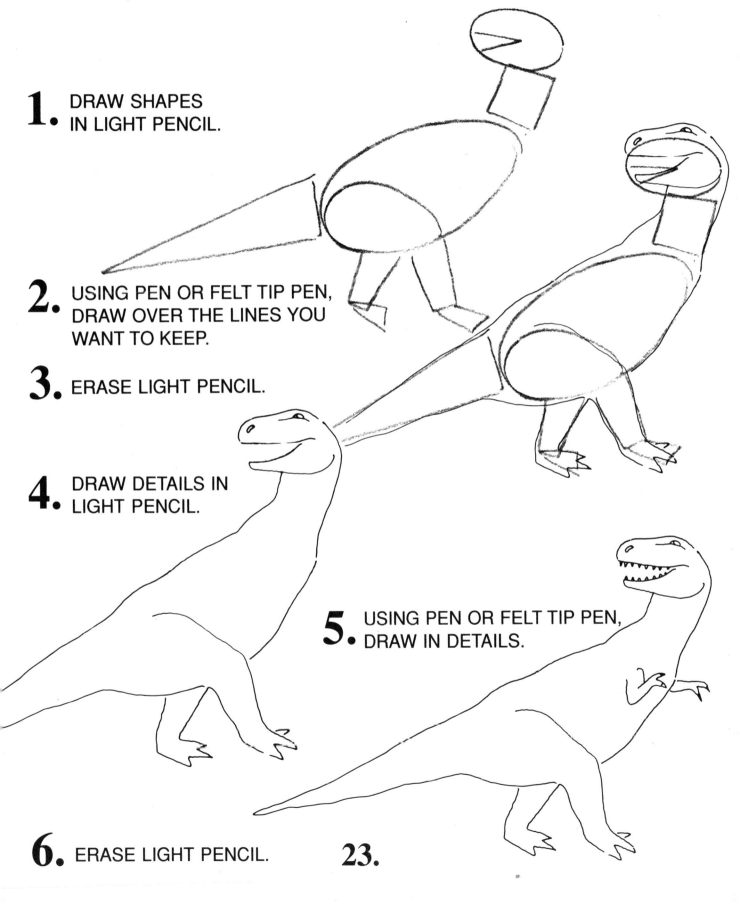

1. DRAW SHAPES IN LIGHT PENCIL.

2. USING PEN OR FELT TIP PEN, DRAW OVER THE LINES YOU WANT TO KEEP.

3. ERASE LIGHT PENCIL.

4. DRAW DETAILS IN LIGHT PENCIL.

5. USING PEN OR FELT TIP PEN, DRAW IN DETAILS.

6. ERASE LIGHT PENCIL.

CASTLES AND DOLLS

1. DRAW SHAPES IN LIGHT PENCIL.

2. USING PEN OR FELT TIP PEN, DRAW OVER THE LINES YOU WANT TO KEEP.

3. ERASE LIGHT PENCIL.

4. DRAW DETAILS IN LIGHT PENCIL.

5. USING PEN OR FELT TIP PEN, DRAW IN DETAILS.

6. ERASE LIGHT PENCIL.

1. DRAW SHAPES IN LIGHT PENCIL.

2. USING PEN OR FELT TIP PEN, DRAW OVER THE LINES YOU WANT TO KEEP.

3. ERASE LIGHT PENCIL.

4. DRAW DETAILS IN LIGHT PENCIL.

5. USING PEN OR FELT TIP PEN, DRAW IN DETAILS.

6. ERASE LIGHT PENCIL.

25.

CAN YOU SEE THE

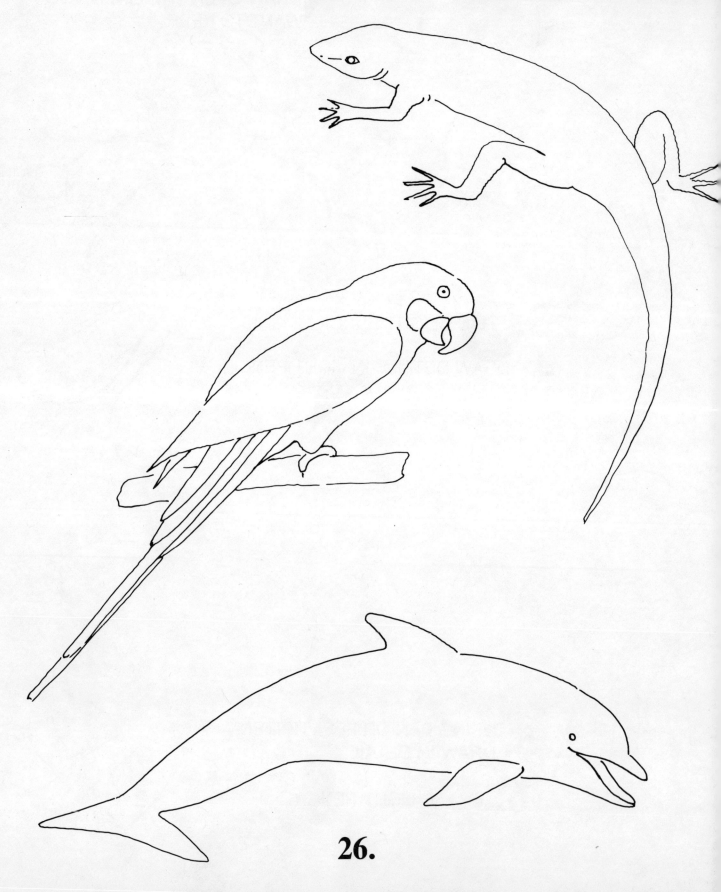

26.

SHAPES

THAT MAKE A
DOLPHIN, UNICORN, LIZARD,
PARROT, JET AND TREE?

SEE NEXT PAGE FOR SHAPES.

27.

28.

3.

TRACING FUN

Tracing is one of the easiest ways to learn how to draw. By tracing over a drawing or photograph, you can see not only the shapes we talked about in chapters one and two, but also something new...dimension.

All objects have three dimensions:

      1. height-how tall it is,

      2. width-how wide it is, and

      3. depth-how deep it is or how far back it goes.

A box has height, width and depth.

The best thing about tracing a drawing or photo is that the object is already in two dimensions: height and width. To draw, you need to be able to see how to change a three-dimensional object to a two-dimensional or a flat picture. Tracing is the best, easiest and fastest way to develop this skill. Chapter three shows how to draw from photos and other drawings.

Remember-**have fun!**

TRACE YOUR FAVORITE CARTOON

1. TAPE CARTOON TO YOUR ART TABLE OR OTHER SMOOTH SURFACE THAT TAPE WILL NOT HARM. (GET PERMISSION IF IT DOESN'T BELONG TO YOU. MASKING TAPE IS SAFEST TO USE.)

2. TAPE TRACING PAPER OVER CARTOON.

3. USING A PEN, PENCIL OR COLORED PENCIL, CAREFULLY DRAW OVER THE LINES YOU WANT TO KEEP.

4. YOU CAN CHANGE DETAILS AS YOU DRAW.

EXAMPLE:

30.

MONSTERS AND SPACESHIPS

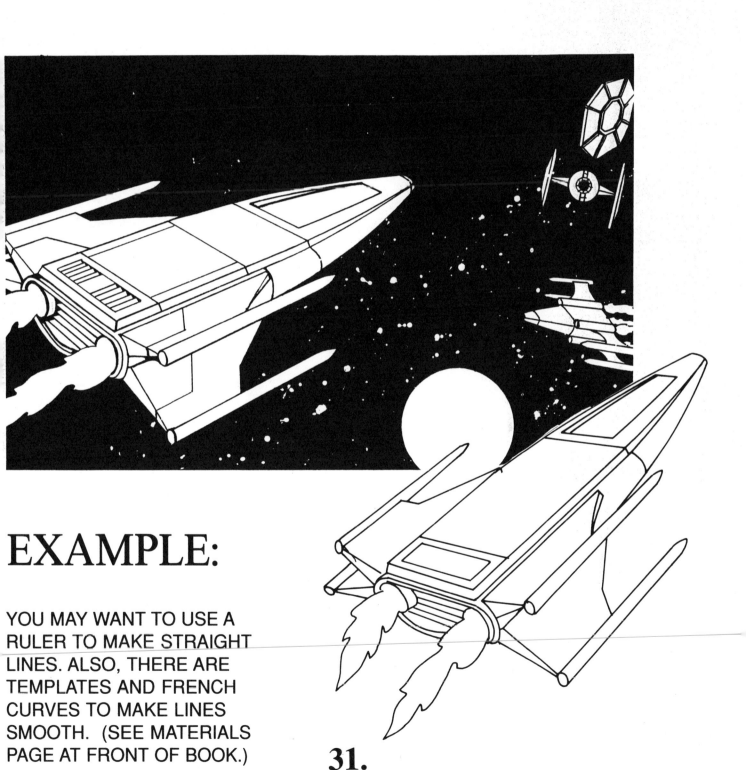

EXAMPLE:

YOU MAY WANT TO USE A RULER TO MAKE STRAIGHT LINES. ALSO, THERE ARE TEMPLATES AND FRENCH CURVES TO MAKE LINES SMOOTH. (SEE MATERIALS PAGE AT FRONT OF BOOK.)

DRAWINGS TO TRACE

1. TAPE DRAWING TO YOUR ART TABLE OR OTHER SMOOTH SURFACE THAT TAPE WILL NOT HARM. (GET PERMISSION IF IT DOESN'T BELONG TO YOU. MASKING TAPE IS SAFEST TO USE.)

2. TAPE TRACING PAPER OVER DRAWING.

3. USING A PEN, PENCIL OR COLORED PENCIL, CARE-FULLY DRAW OVER THE LINES YOU WANT TO KEEP.

4. YOU CAN CHANGE DETAILS AS YOU DRAW.

EXAMPLE:

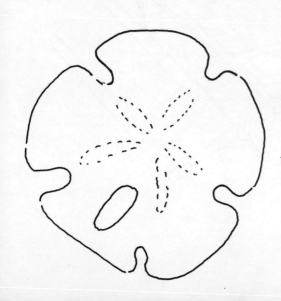  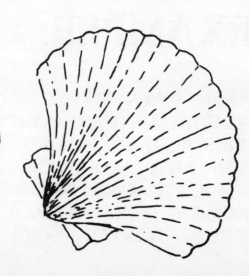

32.

PHOTOS TO TRACE

1. TAPE PHOTO TO YOUR ART TABLE OR OTHER SMOOTH SURFACE THAT TAPE WILL NOT HARM. (GET PERMISSION IF IT DOESN'T BELONG TO YOU. MASKING TAPE IS SAFEST TO USE.)

EXAMPLE:

2. TAPE TRACING PAPER OVER PHOTO.

3. USING A PEN, PENCIL OR COLORED PENCIL, CAREFULLY DRAW OVER THE LINES YOU WANT TO KEEP.

4. YOU CAN CHANGE DETAILS AS YOU DRAW.

PHOTOS TO TRACE

1. TAPE PHOTO TO YOUR ART TABLE OR OTHER SMOOTH SURFACE THAT TAPE WILL NOT HARM. (GET PERMISSION IF IT DOESN'T BELONG TO YOU. MASKING TAPE IS SAFEST TO USE.)

2. TAPE TRACING PAPER OVER PHOTO.

3. USING A PEN, PENCIL OR COLORED PENCIL, CAREFULLY DRAW OVER THE LINES YOU WANT TO KEEP.

4. YOU CAN CHANGE DETAILS AS YOU DRAW.

EXAMPLE

PENCIL ON DRAWING PAPER

1. TAPE PHOTO TO YOUR ART TABLE OR OTHER SMOOTH SURFACE THAT TAPE WILL NOT HARM. (GET PERMISSION IF IT DOESN'T BELONG TO YOU. MASKING TAPE IS SAFEST TO USE.)

2. TAPE TRACING PAPER OVER PHOTO.

3. USING A PEN, PENCIL OR COLORED PENCIL, CAREFULLY DRAW OVER THE LINES YOU WANT TO KEEP.

4. YOU CAN CHANGE DETAILS AS YOU DRAW.

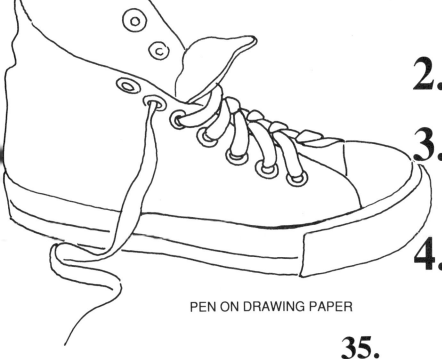

PEN ON DRAWING PAPER

35.

4.

ADVANCED DRAWING

In the previous chapters we have shown how to use shapes to draw or trace from a cartoon, drawing or photo.

Chapter four shows how to draw when tracing is not possible.

Learning to draw from a subject (a person) or an object (a toy or apple, etc.) makes it possible to draw anything you can see.

Using what you have learned about shapes and drawing, you now will learn how to see those shapes in an object or a subject.

This will take practice; practice not only in drawing but practice in seeing.

You probably can easily see the squares in a box. But can you see the triangles and squares in a row of houses? Can you see the circles in an apple?

Once you learn to see shapes in objects you will find it easy to draw anything.

When you can see the detail in an object, you will be able to draw the detail.

You may find you enjoy drawing even more once you learn how to use detail to make your drawings more life like.

DRAW AN APPLE
(START WITH A SIMPLE SHAPE)

1. LOOK CAREFULLY AT YOUR APPLE.

2. DRAW THE BASIC SHAPE IN LIGHT PENCIL.

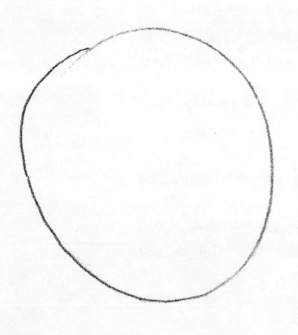

3. LOOK AT YOUR APPLE AGAIN. CAN YOU MAKE THE SHAPE MORE LIKE THE APPLE? DRAW OVER THE BASIC SHAPE AGAIN WITH LIGHT PENCIL. TRY TO MAKE THE SHAPE MORE LIKE THE APPLE.

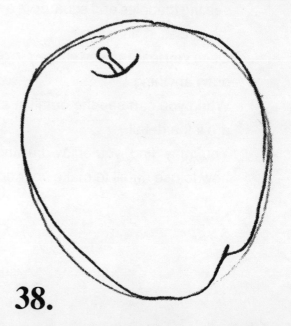

4. LOOK FOR DETAILS. LOOK FOR
TEXTURE - AN APPLE IS SMOOTH.
DRAW THE APPLE'S SHAPE
IN LIGHT PENCIL.

5. LOOK AT THE WHOLE DRAWING.
WHAT SHAPE LOOKS THE BEST?
DRAW OVER THE LINES YOU LIKE
WITH PEN OR FELT TIP.

6. WHAT DETAILS LOOK THE BEST?
DRAW OVER THEM IN PEN OR
FELT TIP.

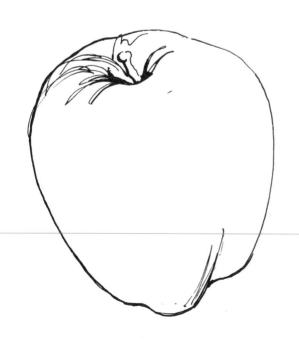

7. ERASE THE PENCIL LINES. (YOU
MAY WANT TO USE TRACING PA-
PER TO TRACE OVER THE DRAW-
ING.)

39.

DRAW A TEDDY BEAR
(THE TEDDY BEAR HAS A FURRY TEXTURE)

1. LOOK CAREFULLY AT YOUR TEDDY BEAR.

2. DRAW THE BASIC SHAPE IN LIGHT PENCIL.

3. LOOK AT YOUR TEDDY BEAR AGAIN. CAN YOU MAKE THE SHAPE MORE LIKE THE TEDDY BEAR? DRAW OVER THE BASIC SHAPE AGAIN WITH LIGHT PEN-CIL. TRY TO MAKE THE SHAPE MORE LIKE THE TEDDY BEAR.

4. LOOK FOR DETAILS. LOOK FOR TEXTURE - A TEDDY BEAR IS FURRY. DRAW THE DETAIL IN LIGHT PENCIL.

EXAMPLES OF WAYS TO DRAW FUR TEXTURES:

5. LOOK AT THE WHOLE DRAWING. WHAT SHAPE LOOKS THE BEST? DRAW OVER THE LINES YOU LIKE WITH PEN OR FELT TIP.

6. WHAT DETAILS LOOK THE BEST? DRAW OVER THEM IN PEN OR FELT TIP.

7. ERASE THE PENCIL LINES. (YOU MAY WANT TO USE TRACING PAPER TO TRACE OVER THE DRAWING.)

41.

DRAW A FRIEND

1. LOOK CAREFULLY AT YOUR FRIEND.

2. DRAW THE BASIC SHAPE IN LIGHT PENCIL.

3. LOOK AT YOUR FRIEND AGAIN. CAN YOU MAKE THE SHAPE MORE LIKE YOUR FRIEND? DRAW OVER THE BASIC SHAPE AGAIN WITH LIGHT PENCIL. TRY TO MAKE THE SHAPE MORE LIKE YOUR FRIEND.

4. LOOK FOR DETAILS. LOOK FOR TEXTURE. DRAW THE DETAIL IN LIGHT PENCIL.

5. LOOK AT THE WHOLE DRAWING. WHAT SHAPE LOOKS THE BEST? DRAW OVER THE LINES YOU LIKE WITH PEN OR FELT TIP.

6. WHAT DETAILS LOOK THE BEST? DRAW OVER THEM IN PEN OR FELT TIP.

7. ERASE THE PENCIL LINES. (YOU MAY WANT TO USE TRACING PAPER TO TRACE OVER THE DRAWING.)

44.

5.

SHADING

Adding shadows and shading to your drawing gives it texture and makes it more life like.

In this chapter we will show you how to use pencil, charcoal, and pens to give your drawing shading. You decide - do you want the detail light or dark?

By learning about a light source (where the lighting is coming from), you will quickly learn how to determine where a shadow should go.

From this point on, we encourage you to take your time, learn to really see what is around you. Most likely, the more life like your drawings are the more you will enjoy creating them.

And remember - **have fun!**

PENCIL, CHARCOAL,

HOW TO USE YOUR PENCIL, CHARCOAL OR PEN FOR SHADING.

WHEN USING PENCIL, YOU MIGHT WANT TO USE SKETCHING PAPER OR PAPER WITH TEXTURE.

HOLD SOFT LEADED PENCIL SO YOU ARE USING THE SIDE OF THE LEAD. USE LESS PRESSURE FOR LIGHTER SHADING AND MORE PRESSURE FOR DARKER SHADING.

PENCIL

DARK   MEDIUM   LIGHT

TRY THIS - MAKE DIFFERENT VALUES - FROM DARK TO LIGHT

WHEN USING CHARCOAL, YOU MIGHT WANT TO USE CHARCOAL PAPER OR PAPER WITH SOME TEXTURE.

HOLD CHARCOAL ON SIDE. USE LESS PRESSURE FOR LIGHTER SHADING AND MORE PRESSURE FOR DARKER SHADING.

CHARCOAL

DARK   MEDIUM   LIGHT

TRY THIS - MAKE DIFFERENT VALUES - FROM DARK TO LIGHT.

46.

OR PEN

YOU CAN USE A PEN TO DRAW LINES FOR SHADING. THE CLOSER TOGETHER THE LINES, THE DARKER IT LOOKS; THE FARTHER APART THE LINES, THE LIGHTER IT LOOKS.

TRY THIS:

LIGHT   MEDIUM   DARK

YOU CAN ALSO CROSS THE LINES TO MAKE IT APPEAR DARKER;

TRY THIS:

LIGHT   MEDIUM   DARK

WITH PEN YOU MIGHT WANT TO TRY DIFFER-ENT TYPES OF PAPERS AND SEE WHAT SUR-FACE YOU LIKE THE BEST.

PEN

SHADOWS AND

LIGHT SOURCE

DRAW AN APPLE.
PUT IN SHADOWS BY
SHADING WITH A PENCIL,
CHARCOAL, OR PEN.

KNOW YOUR LIGHT SOURCE.

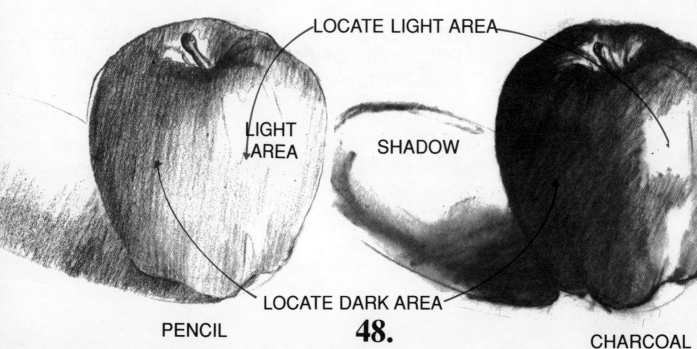

LOCATE LIGHT AREA

LIGHT
AREA

SHADOW

LOCATE DARK AREA

PENCIL

48.

CHARCOAL

SHADING

LIGHT SOURCE

DRAW A JAR OR CUP.
PUT IN SHADOWS BY
SHADING WITH A PENCIL, PEN OR
CHARCOAL.

KNOW YOUR LIGHT SOURCE.

LOCATE DARK AREA

PEN

LOCATE LIGHT AREA

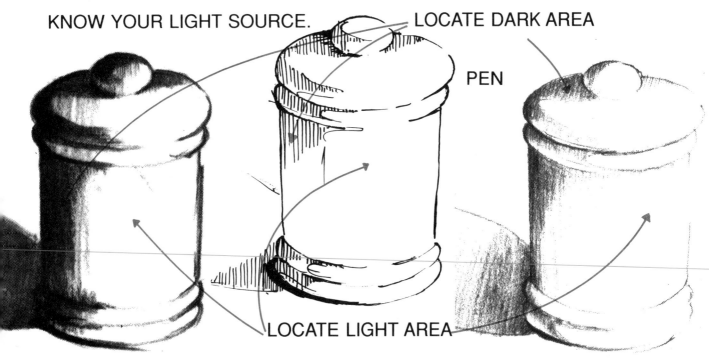

CHARCOAL

49.

PENCIL

SHADING AND TEXTURES

KNOW YOUR LIGHT SOURCE

SHADING A HILLSIDE WITH PENCIL
YOU CAN SHOW DIFFERENT TEX-
TURES THAT LOOK LIKE GRASS
AND BUSHES.

SHADING A HILLSIDE WITH CHAR-
COAL YOU CAN SHOW DIFFERENT
TEXTURES THAT LOOK LIKE
GRASS AND BUSHES.

SHADING A HILLSIDE WITH PEN
YOU CAN SHOW DIFFERENT TEX
TURES THAT LOOK LIKE GRASS
AND BUSHES.

DRAW A HILLSIDE

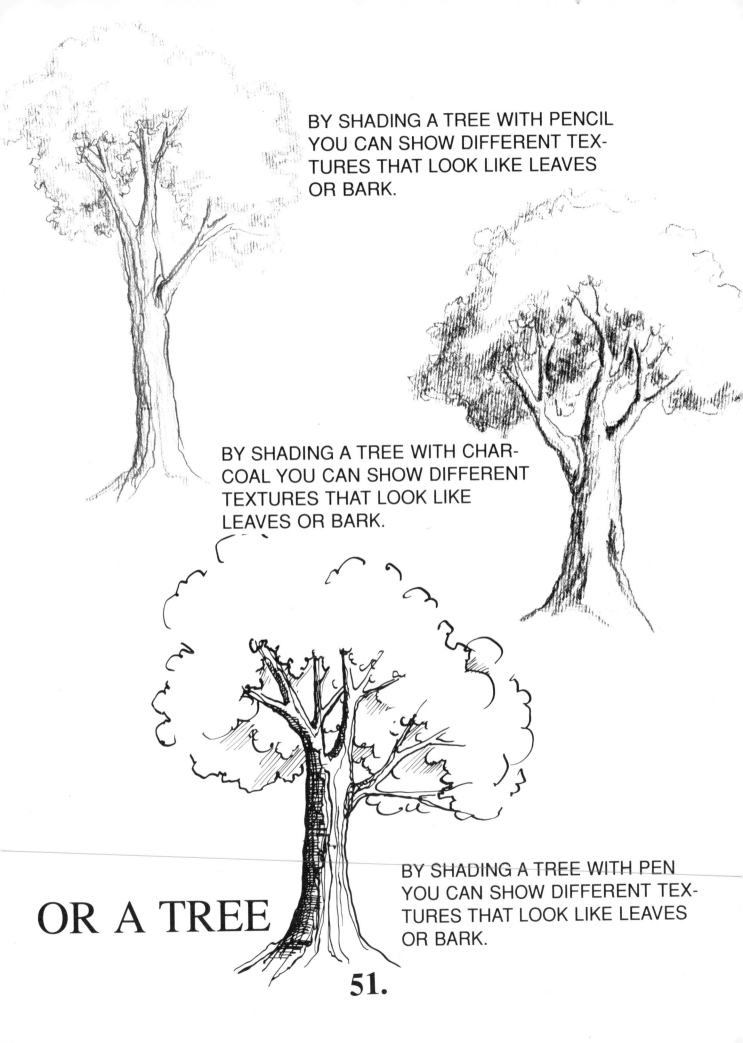

BY SHADING A TREE WITH PENCIL
YOU CAN SHOW DIFFERENT TEX-
TURES THAT LOOK LIKE LEAVES
OR BARK.

BY SHADING A TREE WITH CHAR-
COAL YOU CAN SHOW DIFFERENT
TEXTURES THAT LOOK LIKE
LEAVES OR BARK.

OR A TREE

BY SHADING A TREE WITH PEN
YOU CAN SHOW DIFFERENT TEX-
TURES THAT LOOK LIKE LEAVES
OR BARK.

51.

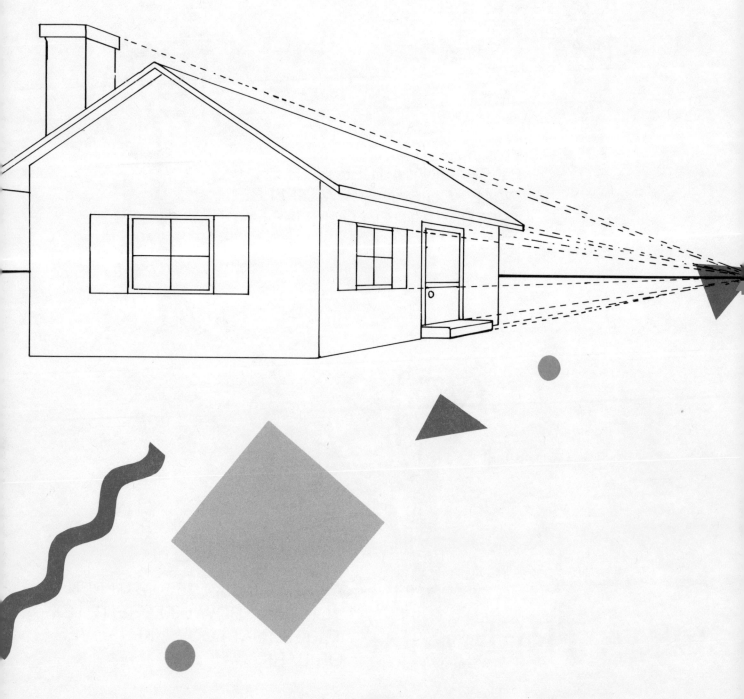

52.

6.

PERSPECTIVE

Perspective is used to make a flat (two-dimensional) picture look life like (three-dimensional).

One way to show perspective is by making the object or subject closest to you larger. If you make other objects smaller, they will look further away. To help you understand, we will show you easy ways to use one point perspective. We will also show you a horizon line and a vanishing point. It sounds hard, but it isn't!

These skills will help you understand why a railroad track seems to vanish into the distance. The more you understand about perspective, the more your drawings will look life like. Perspective is more difficult to understand than what you've already learned. So be patient and remember - **have fun!**

PUT PERSPECTIVE IN

OBJECTS FURTHER
AWAY ARE SMALLER

PEN ON DRAWING PAPER

54.

YOUR DRAWINGS

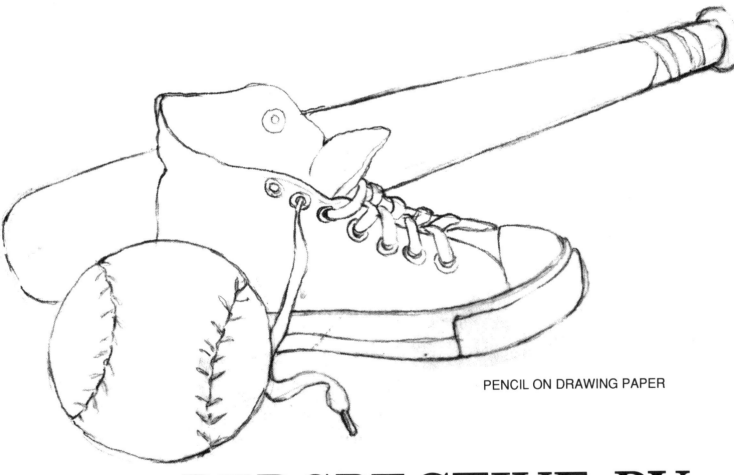

PENCIL ON DRAWING PAPER

PERSPECTIVE BY OVERLAPPING

ONE POINT PERSPECTIVE

1. DRAW A HORIZON (OR HORIZONTAL) LINE.
2. DRAW IN AN X WHERE YOU WANT YOUR POINT.
3. DRAW A SQUARE.

EXAMPLE:

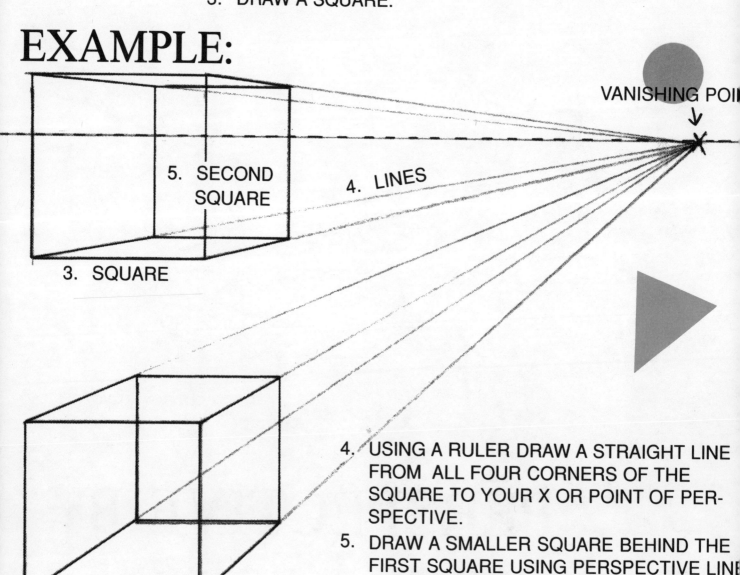

VANISHING POIN

5. SECOND SQUARE

4. LINES

3. SQUARE

4. USING A RULER DRAW A STRAIGHT LINE FROM ALL FOUR CORNERS OF THE SQUARE TO YOUR X OR POINT OF PERSPECTIVE.
5. DRAW A SMALLER SQUARE BEHIND THE FIRST SQUARE USING PERSPECTIVE LINE
6. ERASE OVERLAPPING LINES BEHIND BOX YOU NOW HAVE A THREE-DIMENSIONAL BOX.

CAN YOU SEE THE HORIZON LINE AND THE
POINT OF PERSPECTIVE IN THIS PHOTO?

EXAMPLE:

VANISHING POINT

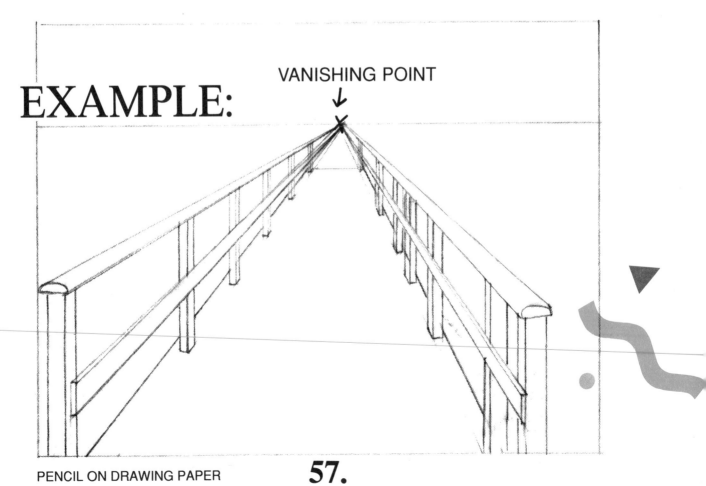

HOUSES IN A ROW

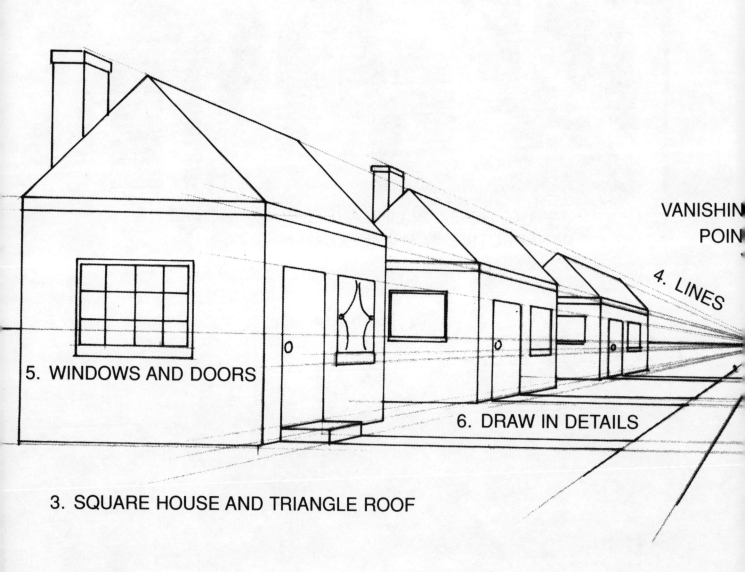

VANISHIN
POIN

4. LINES

5. WINDOWS AND DOORS

6. DRAW IN DETAILS

3. SQUARE HOUSE AND TRIANGLE ROOF

1. DRAW A HORIZON (OR HORIZONTAL) LINE.
2. DRAW IN AN X WHERE YOU WANT YOUR POINT.
3. DRAW A SQUARE HOUSE AND DRAW A TRIANGLE ROOF ON TOP.
4. USING A RULER, DRAW A STRAIGHT LINE FROM ALL THE POINTS (CORNERS) ON ONE SIDE OF THE HOUSE TO THE X OR VANISHING POINT
5. DRAW IN DETAILS (DOORS AND WINDOWS, ETC.) USING YOUR PERSPECTIVE LINES.

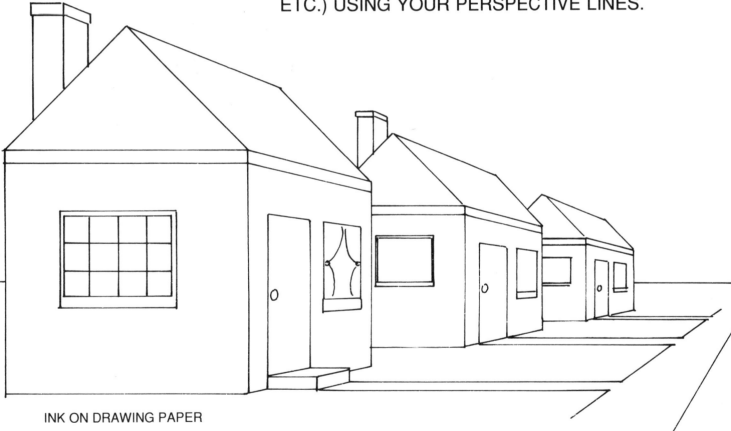

INK ON DRAWING PAPER

6. ERASE LINES YOU DONT WANT. YOU NOW HAVE A THREE-DIMENSIONAL ROW OF HOUSES.

59.

A DAY IN THE COUNTRY...

CHARCOAL ON CHARCOAL PAPER

INK ON ILLUSTRATION BOARD

OR A CITY SCENE..

61.

OUT BY THE OCEAN...

PENCIL ON DRAWING PAPER

INK ON DRAWING PAPER

OR CASTLES WITH KINGS AND QUEENS!

63.